D1826891

T O

F R O M

Other Helen Exley giftbooks:
I Love You   Passion
The Kiss   Love Letters

Published simultaneously in 1999 by Exley Publications Ltd in Great Britain and Exley Publications LLC in the USA.

Concept development by Lincoln Exley
Illustrations and anthology © Lincoln Exley Designs Ltd 1999
© Exley Publications Ltd 1999
Illustrations by Cathie Felstead.
Edited by Andrew Maxwell Hislop.

12 11 10 9 8 7 6 5 4 3 2 1

ISBN 1-86187-177-5

A copy of the CIP data is available from the British Library on request. All rights reserved. No part of this publication may be reproduced or transmitted in any form or by any means, electronic or mechanical, including photocopy, recording or any information storage and retrieval system without permission in writing from the Publisher.

To Paul, love Cathie

ACKNOWLEDGEMENTS: Lincoln Exley Designs are grateful for permission to reproduce copyright material. Whilst every effort has been made to trace copyright holders, L. E. D. would be happy to hear from any not here acknowledged. E.E. CUMMINGS: "i like my body when it is with your" and "may i feel said he" reprinted from Complete Poems 1904-1962, by E.E. Cummings, ed. by George J. Firmage, by permission of W.W. Norton. © 1991 by the Trustees for the E.E. Cummings Trust and George J. Firmage. JOHNNY MERCER: From "Too Marvelous For Words". © Warner Chappell Music Inc. BRIAN PATTEN: From "Party Piece" from Little Johnny's Confession. Reprinted by permission of HarperCollins Publishers Ltd. BESSIE SMITH: From "Empty Bed Blues" (Part 1 and 2). © Record Music Publishing Company.

Exley Publications Ltd, 16 Chalk Hill, Watford, Herts WD1 4BN, UK.
Exley Publications LLC, 232 Madison Avenue, Suite 1409, NY 10016, USA.
Lincoln Exley Designs, Suite 4, Kings Court, 153 High St, Watford, Herts WD1 2ER, UK.

A Book of
HEARTS

Love.

It's unfathomable. It's inexplicable.

It's a miracle.

EXLEY
NEW YORK • WATFORD, UK

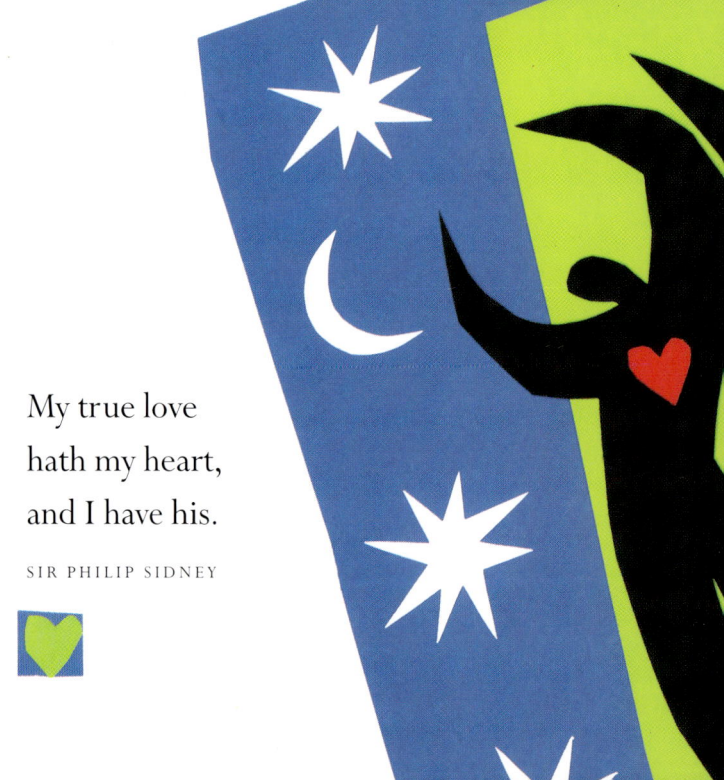

My true love
hath my heart,
and I have his.

SIR PHILIP SIDNEY

... let there be spaces
in your togetherness,
And let the winds
of the heavens dance
between you.

KAHLIL GIBRAN

She walks in beauty, like the night
Of cloudless climes and starry skies.

LORD BYRON

Wild night!
Wild nights
Were I with thee
Wild nights should be
Our luxury.

EMILY DICKINSON

If I never met you
I would have dreamed you into being.

SEBASTIAN CHANTOIX

Love conquers all things.

VIRGIL

Love is king.

MARK THORNICROFT

Love conquers all things
— except poverty and toothache.

MAE WEST

How do I love thee? Let me count the ways.
I love thee to the depth and breadth and height
My soul can reach....

ELIZABETH BARRETT BROWNING

My heart has made its mind up
And I'm afraid it's you.

WENDY COPE

The eskimos
have fifty-two names for snow
because it is important to them;
there ought to be
as many for love.

MARGARET ATWOOD

Erotic love
is the spindle
on which the
earth turns.

OCTAVIO PAZ

But let's unclip our
minds
And let tumble free
The mad, mangled
crocodile of love.

BRIAN PATTEN

To love and to be loved
is to feel the sun from both sides.
DAVID VISCOTT

Life is a flower
of which love is the honey.
VICTOR HUGO

Love comforteth like the sunshine after rain.
WILLIAM SHAKESPEARE

The pain of loving you is almost more
than I can bear.

D H LAWRENCE

One is very crazy in love.

SIGMUND FREUD

Love's… a pardonable insanity.

SEBASTIAN CHANTOIX

Love is an act of endless forgiveness.

PETER USTINOV

Kindness in words creates confidence.
Kindness in thinking creates profoundness.
Kindness in giving creates love.

LAO-TZU

*The ultimate test of a relationship is to disagree
but to hold hands.*

ALEXANDRA PENNEY

The madness of love
is the greatest of
heaven's blessings.

PLATO

*The heart that loves
is always young.*
PETER USTINOV

*Love is the greatest
refreshment in life.*
PABLO PICASSO

may i feel said he
(i'll squeal said she
just once said he)
it's fun said she.

E E CUMMINGS

i like my body
when it is with your body.

E E CUMMINGS

When my bed is empty,
Makes me feel awful mean and blue.
My springs are getting rusty,
Living single like I do.

BESSIE SMITH

Love becomes
the ultimate answer
to the ultimate
human question.

ARCHIBALD MACLEISH

Two human loves make one divine.

ELIZABETH BARRETT BROWNING

Love is of all the passions the strongest,
for it attacks simultaneously the head,
the heart and the senses.

VOLTAIRE

Drink to me only with thine eyes,
And I will pledge with mine.

BEN JONSON

The last of your kisses was ever the sweetest;
the last smile the brightest.

JOHN KEATS

We know things better through love
than through knowledge.

UMBERTO ECO

To love a thing means wanting it to live....

CONFUCIUS

You're much too marvelous,
Too marvelous for words.

JOHNNY MERCER

Love is something eternal – the aspect may change, but not the essence.

VINCENT VAN GOGH

... each day I love you more,
Today more than yesterday and less
than tomorrow.

ROSEMONDE GERARD

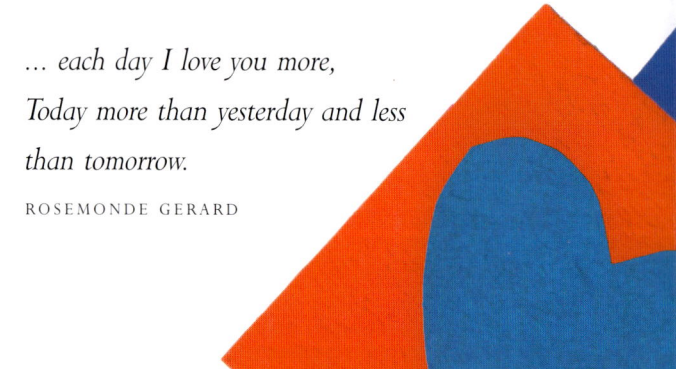

ABOUT THE ARTIST

The creator of the Hearts range is Cathie Felstead
who uses paper cuts to illustrate love quotes
from some of the world's greatest minds
with simple abstract designs and strong jazzy colours.
Cathie takes particular inspiration from Paul Klee's
use of symbols and shapes that create images at once
fragile and powerful, Auguste Macke and Franz Marc's
stunning bright colours that seem to jump off the
canvas and Matisse's brilliantly simple, yet
sophisticated graphic compositions.

Cathie was educated in the Netherlands at
Akademie Artibus, in the UK at Chelsea School of
Art (BA [Hons]), and at the Royal College of Art
(MA [RCA]). She is a multi-faceted artist producing
corporate work for ICI, British Airways, The Body
Shop and Fiat, illustration for numerous children's
books, art in Harpers and Queen, Vogue,
The Sunday Times and set design for the Ballet
Rambert and Channel 4 TV.